# EFFECTIVE GRANT WRITING

Submit a Stronger Application

## Angie R. Boecker

ISBN-13: 978-0692378571
ISBN-10: 069237857X

# DEDICATION

This book is dedicated to my husband and my parents. The three people I can count on no matter what happens in life.

# CONTENTS

# ACKNOWLEDGMENT

Thank you Leslie Ann H. for you encouragement and support. Thank you Diane W. for the advice.

*Effective Grant Writing: Submit a Stronger Application* provides you common sense tips for submitting a stronger grant application. *Effective Grant Writing: Submit a Stronger Application* is directed toward organizations but anyone can benefit from the information. Keep in mind that because there are so many factors that affect the grant process, nothing can guarantee funding of a grant application; however, utilizing the tips in *Effective Grant Writing: Submit a Stronger Application* will help you submit your best application. Good luck in your grant writing adventures!

Angie

# INTRODUCTION

Have you ever thought about what it would be like to write down the information you learned on the job and share it with others with the hope that it will help them? I did. One day I decided to do just that. This is when *Effective Grant Writing: Submit a Stronger Application* was born.

For over seven years I worked as the Grants Specialist for a grantmaking organization that gave grants (and scholarships) to nonprofit organizations, individuals, high school seniors, schools and government units. Part of my job was conducting intake on all submitted grant applications ensuring applicant eligibility, guideline compliance and application completeness.

In this position, I answered a lot of questions; explained grant programs; shared tips that helped applicants improve their applications; explained to applicants why their application was not funded; described grant obligations to recipients; and reported constituent/project statistical data and grant impacts to a State agency.

In addition to working for that grantmaking organization, I co-managed a broadband project for a county economic development department. In this role, I was involved in managing the project budget; acted as a liaison between the economic development department and project contractors; reported about project outcomes and impacts plus prepared for the final project audit. This experience allowed me to write *Effective Grant Writing: Submit a Stronger Application* not only from the grantmaking organization's perspective, but also from the perspective of a grant administrator.

*Effective Grant Writing: Submit a Stronger Application* is packed with information that answers commonly asked questions such as:

- What are grants?
- Why apply for a grant?
- Do I have to repay grant funds?
- Where do I find grants?
- Who creates grant programs? Aren't they all alike?
- What happens after an application is submitted to a grantmaking organization?
- How strict are the application deadlines?
- What is the difference between a goal and an outcome?
- Do I always have to submit a budget with a grant application? How do I create a budget for the application?
- My application was funded! Now what?

Along with answering these commonly asked question I made sure that *Effective Grant Writing: Submit a Stronger Application* provided information that helps you, the grant writer, avoid some of the frequent mistakes I saw writers make when writing their proposal narrative and submitting their grant applications (or administering grants). Mistakes that included:

- Not preparing in advance to write and submit the application
- Neglecting to thoroughly read the program guidelines or application questions
- Not following instructions
- Attaching a confusing and unclear budget page with the application
- Not planning or fully explaining the goals for the project being proposed
- Submitting an application that had the evaluators guessing as to the intent of the project or questioning the relevance or merit of the project/budget items
- Not submitting progress/final reports for previously funded grants

Grants are a great source of support, they can be highly competitive and nothing can guarantee funding of a grant application. For these reasons, the ability to submit a strong grant application is valuable. A strong application starts with understanding the granting process and the expectations of grantmaking organizations and evaluators. Whether you are new to grant writing or you have written a few grant applications, *Effective Grant Writing: Submit a Stronger Application* will give you an understanding of that process and those expectations. It is filled with tips that will help you submit your best application. Tips such as:

- Laying a good foundation before beginning the application process
- Using the program guidelines and final report form to your advantage
- Meeting application deadlines
- Creating a well thought out proposal narrative by using a step by step process for setting/explaining proposal goals
- Developing a budget page for the application
- Maximizing draft reviews and proofreading the narrative
- Identifying grant obligations and meeting reporting requirement

As you read *Effective Grant Writing: Submit a Stronger Application* you will discover that the preparation you do before completing the application is just as important as actually writing the proposal narrative.

*Thank you for choosing this book and enjoy exploring all the information it contains.*

# CHAPTER ONE

# GETTING STARTED

Grants provide funds to schools, government units, 501(c)3 non-profit organizations or sometimes individuals, businesses and non-exempt organizations using a fiscal agent. (A fiscal agent is a 501(c)3 organization that sponsors a project being coordinated by a non-exempt organization.)

Typically, organizations apply for grants when they want to:
- Expand their programs
- Strengthen their organization with staff trainings, strategic planning or board/organizational development
- Conduct a project that will help people in their community
- Make capital purchases
- Pay general operating expenses

*Do I have to repay grant funds?*
Grant funds generally do not have to be paid back; however, there are a few circumstances where repayment may be required. Examples include:
- The funded project (event, purchase, training, etc.) did not occur
- The *actual* project revenue at the end of the project was high enough that the grant was not necessary
- Grant obligations were not met (More in Chapter 6)
- Illegal activities occurred
- Misrepresentation on a grant application

*What is the difference between a grant and a scholarship?*
The main difference between a grant and a scholarship is a scholarship is generally awarded to students for financial aid and a grant is awarded to non-profits, government units, etc.

*Where do I find grants?*
Finding legitimate grant programs that you are eligible for is not always easy. Contacting foundations in your area is a good place to start your search. (In general, foundations are nonprofit organizations that give grants to other nonprofits.) If they do not offer a grant you can take advantage of, they may be able to provide you with resources.

### Grant Program Development
*Who creates grant programs? Aren't they all alike?*
Not all grant programs are created the same. Most grantmaking organizations develop their own grant programs. They determine program components such as:
- What type of program they will offer
- Who will be eligible to apply to that program
- What types of projects are eligible for funding
- How much the maximum grant amount will be

Grant program development may also include creating the:
- Program guidelines
- Grant application
- Grant contract
- Final reporting requirements

Some programs are simple and others are more complex depending, in part, on the type of program and the potential amount of the grant. Another factor that might influence how a program is developed is the source of the money used to fund the program.

Typically, grantmaking organizations receive the funds they

disperse to their constituents from an outside source such as a private benefactor, the State Legislator or a Federal governing body. These sources sometimes dictate how the grantmaking organization uses the funds.

---

### TIP

Because grant programs, applications and grantmaking organizations are not the same and each has different requirements, adapt the information provided in the following pages to fit each.

---

### Granting Process

*What happens after an application is submitted to a grantmaking organization?*

The simple answer is that it depends on the grantmaking organization. Because some grantmaking organizations receive only a few dozen applications in one grant round and others can receive a couple hundred, each organization has different procedures in place for processing submitted applications.

The number of applications a grantmaking organization receives depends on the size of the grantmaking organization and the region they serve. Some grantmaking organizations serve only a few counties, while others serve an entire State. There are even some that serve the entire United States.

The process could look something like this:

1. *Intake*: During intake of submitted applications, a staff member ensures applicant eligibility, guideline compliance and application completeness. Some grantmaking organizations allow staff members to deny an application if it is not eligible or is incomplete.

2. *Review*: After intake is complete, staff turns the applications over to evaluators for review. Review might be conducted during an in-person meeting or online.

   Evaluators might consist of:
   - The grantmaking organization's board members
   - An advisory panel made up of volunteer community members
   - Staff members of the grantmaking organization

   If an advisory panel or staff members review the applications, they may not actually be able to approve the applications for funding. They may make recommendations to the Board who will then approve or deny those recommendations.

3. *Approved or Denied*: After the review, grantmaking organizations might notify applicants about the status of their application by calling them, mailing/emailing them a letter or by posting the results online. After notification, some grantmaking organizations send a grant contract to each approved applicant explaining their obligations. The appropriate person (or people) will need to sign this contract and return it to the grantmaking organization. (Some contracts might be electronic; requiring an electronic signature.)

### *Laying a Foundation*

Grant writing can sometimes be an involved process. Getting started right involves laying a foundation for submitting a stronger grant application. Laying a foundation starts with gathering three main documents:
1. Program guidelines
2. Program final report form
3. Application checklist

## Program Guidelines

Typically, grantmaking organizations create program guidelines (sometimes called a fact sheet) to help grant researchers and grant writers understand the purpose of a program and the eligibility requirements. Some grantmakers also include information about eligible and ineligible expenses/proposals and review criteria that evaluators use when reviewing submitted applications.

Examples of review criteria:

- *Value*: Is the project worthy of funding? Is the project/organization unique or does it stand out over others similar to it? How does the project fit with the missions of both the applicant organization and the grantmaking organization?
- *Need for the project*: What is the financial need or community need for the project?
- *Ability to carry out the proposed project*: Does key personnel/volunteers have the knowledge and skills to carry out the project? Does the applicant organization have the ability to pay the project expenses if they exceed the grant amount?

Thoroughly reading the program guidelines will benefit you as you move through the application process.

## Final Report Form

Most grantmaking organizations require grantees to submit some type of final report at the end of the project. (More about final reports in Chapter 6). Usually, final reporting on a funded project is the job of the Project Manager, Executive Director or other person administering the grant; however, obtaining this form as you begin the application process is important because it will help you draft a more results-oriented application. It will tell you more about the outcomes the grantmaking organization will be looking for at the end of the project.

## Application Checklist

The application process can be long so utilizing an application checklist provides you a way to double check your work after completing the application. Sometimes a checklist can be found at the end of the application, within the guidelines or may be available through the grantmaking organization. If the grantmaking organization does not supply one then create one.

To create a checklist, use the guidelines, application questions/instructions, review criteria and final report form. It is not necessary to create a complete checklist right away. You can build the checklist as you go through the application process. This checklist should include items that need to be submitted with the application or tasks that need to be done to ensure guideline compliance and application completeness.

Items on the checklist will differ depending on the requirements of the grantmaking organization, evaluators, grant program and the application questions/instructions.

Examples of checklist items include:

- ☐ All dates within the application are correct
- ☐ All progress/final reports due to the grantmaking organization for previous grants have been submitted
- ☐ The required templates were used (More in Chapter 2)
- ☐ Expenses listed in the budget are explained (More about budgets in Chapter 4)
- ☐ Math calculations are shown in the budget and are accurate
- ☐ All supporting materials relevant to the proposal have been included. (Examples: key personnel bio(s), evidence of community support or an example of past marketing materials)

**KEEP IN MIND**

Building a stronger grant application starts with laying a good foundation. Use the guidelines to get educated about the program, the final report form to look at the end-result and the application checklist to double check your work.

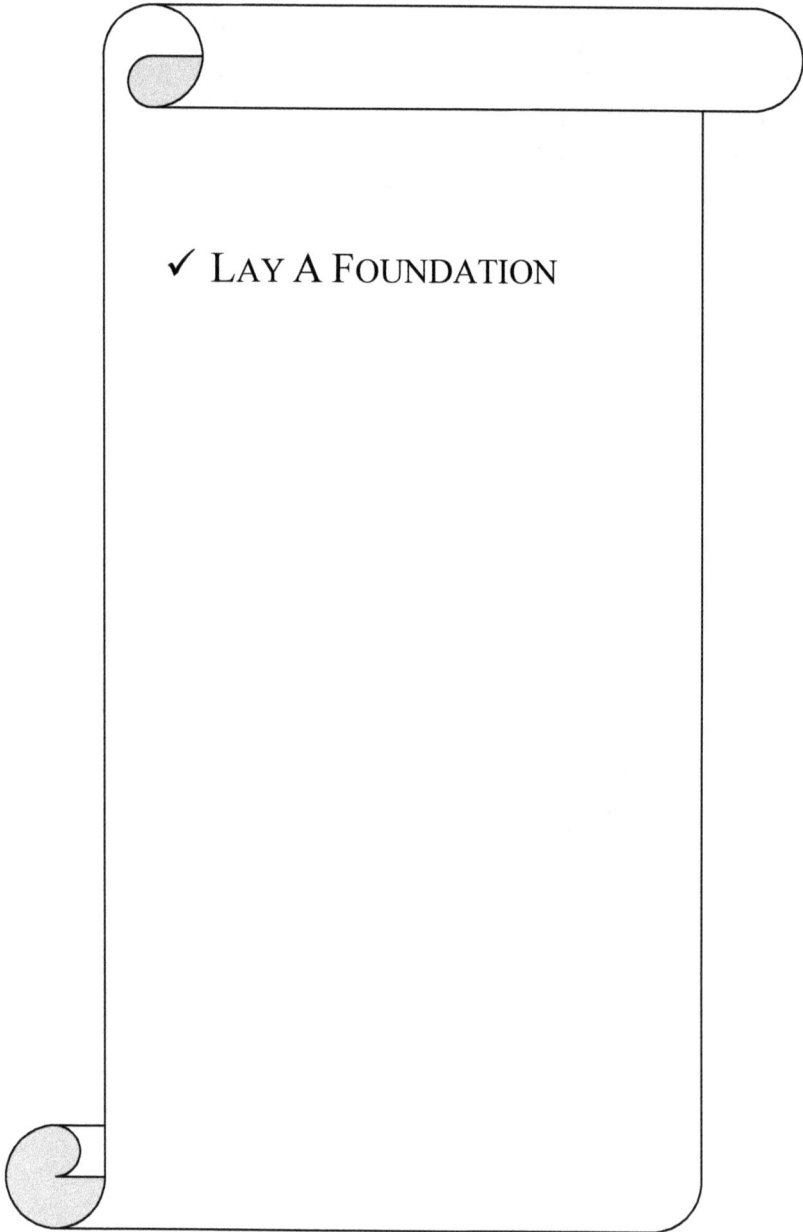

✓ LAY A FOUNDATION

# CHAPTER TWO

# APPLICATION
# BASICS

It is easy to get caught up in writing the proposal narrative; however, to submit a stronger application you must not overlook these five application basics for each grant program you apply to:

## Basic #1 – Application Deadline (Date and Time)

*How strict are the application deadlines?*

Grantmaking organizations usually establish deadlines for all or most of their grant programs. If the grantmaking organization you are applying to has deadlines for their programs they probably are not flexible on those deadlines and will not accept applications after the deadline date and time no matter the circumstances.

Whether you are submitting the application online or on paper, a good rule of thumb is to submit the application well before the deadline. Some things to keep in mind:

- When preparing a grant application online it is a good practice to submit the application during the grantmaking organization's business hours in case there is a problem completing or submitting the application. (Especially if you waited until the deadline date.) Issues such as Internet server problems or documents that are too large for the application upload fields can prevent you from completing or submitting the application. Submitting the application when the grantmaking organization is open allows you to get help with issues that arise.

- When submitting a paper application, make sure you know if the application packet actually has to be in the grantmaking organization's office by the deadline or just postmarked by the deadline.
- When mailing the application packet, use a mailing method that will allow you to prove the mailing and delivery dates.
- While it is always nice to be optimistic, you need to be realistic too. Things happen…the mail is not always on time or, if you are hand delivering the packet, your car might not start, you or your kids might get sick, there might be a blizzard or other bad storm, an emergency might arise that you have to deal with, etc. Sometimes circumstances are out of your control.

## Basic #2 – Contact Person
*Who should be listed as the contact person on the application?*
The person listed on the application as the contact person should be able to answer questions about the project plus handle grant contract and outcome reporting issues if the grant is funded. The person in charge of the project or applicant organization should be listed as the contact person.

## Basic #3 – Application Questions and Instructions
Because grant applications can be a little overwhelming it is important to read the application questions and instructions thoroughly. Not answering a question appropriately or completely (or following the instructions) can result in the application being scored lower or disqualified during intake or review.

Examples of items to watch for:
- *File format* (.pdf, .jpg, .doc, .tiff, etc.): Some grantmaking organizations require that documents be uploaded to online applications in a certain format.

- *Text formatting*: Are you allowed to use paragraph returns or bullets? Are there any line spacing or font size requirements?

- *Compound questions*: A question might be a compound question asking, for example, who and why. Some people may only read enough of the question to answer the "who" component and miss the "why" component. Example question: *"Who will be involved in the project and why were they chosen?"*

## Basic #4 – *Consistency*

If you must supply information such as dates, dollar amounts, locations of events or addresses in more than one place within the application make sure this information is consistent and accurate throughout the application including any attached documents.

Inconsistency or inaccuracy can happen when copying and pasting verbiage from past grant applications (or other documents) or when you have team members working on different sections of the application. Double check all sections for consistency and accuracy before submitting the application.

## Basic #5 – Document Templates

*Do I have to use the templates provided with the application?*
*Why can't I just create my own documents?*

Grantmaking organizations use templates for consistency; ensuring they collect all the information they need to compare your application to another. If the grantmaking organization provides templates such as a budget page template, signature page template or reference form template be sure to use them and not create your own document(s).

**KEEP IN MIND**

Avoid having evaluators score an application lower during review or deny it by:

- Meeting all deadlines
- Following the program guidelines or instructions
- Answering questions appropriately and completely
- Using required templates

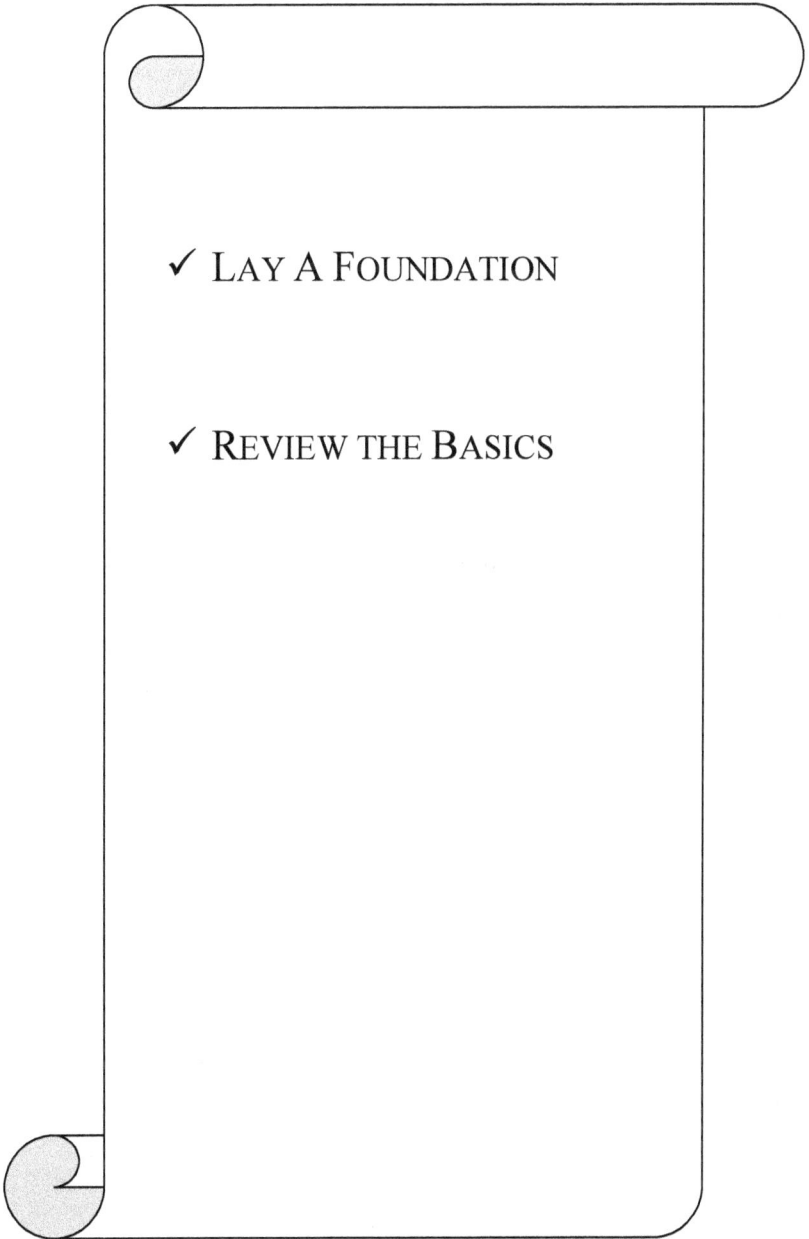

✓ LAY A FOUNDATION

✓ REVIEW THE BASICS

CHAPTER THREE

# HEART OF
# THE APPLICATION

N ow that you have laid the foundation and started building on it by becoming aware of the application basics, it is time to move into the heart of the application. The heart of the application is the narrative explaining the project goal(s) (or objectives) and the expected outcomes (or results).

### *Goals vs. Outcomes*
*What is the difference between a goal and an outcome?*
Merriam-Webster.com defines a goal as *"something that you are trying to do or achieve"*. They define an outcome as *"something that happens as a result of an activity or process"*. In other words, goals are the target and outcomes are what happens when you hit that target.

### *Clarify Proposal Goals and Outcomes*
Before writing the narrative, you (and the person/people in charge of the project *and* administering the grant) must clarify the goal(s) (targets) and expected outcomes for the project you are proposing. Doing this ahead of time, will help you create a well thought out proposal.

After you have clarified the goals and expected outcomes for the project, refer to the program guidelines, application and final report form and make sure your newly constructed goals address the:

- Review criteria
- Application questions
- End-result(s) the grantmaking organization will expect

---

*TIP*

The process of clarifying the project goals may provide you an opportunity to add tasks to your application checklist.

---

### *Guidelines for Goal Setting and Achievement*

Goals set structure and provide direction. When done properly, goals help you achieve more and enable you to measure success. Whether your goals are personal or they are related to a grant proposal, the principles are the same. To successfully set and achieve goals, use the following five guidelines:

1. Write the goal
2. Have desire
3. Visualize the goal as achieved and be detailed
4. Create an action plan
5. Take action

### Guideline #1 – *Write the goal*

*Why do I need to write the goal(s) when I can just remember it?*

Think about a To Do List...writing a To Do List gives you a guide; a way to see what you have accomplished and what you still need to do. Writing a goal reinforces it in your mind and gives you something concrete to refer back to when needed.

### Guideline #2 – *Desire*

All goals must start with desire (or purpose), the "why" for achieving the goal. Desire is what drives goals to a successful conclusion (or outcome). Not having a "why" is like going on a 500-mile road trip and not filling your car with gas. Without fuel, it is unlikely that you will reach the original destination. Without a "why" for your goal you will lose momentum.

When writing the goal(s) for your project you must determine why you want to carry it out. Maybe the project will:

- Provide a creative/effective solution to a problem
- Transform how something is currently being done
- Enhance something and move it to the next level
- Enable people to experience something they normally would not be able to experience
- Fill an ongoing need in the community

## Guideline #3 – Visualize and Be Detailed

Written goals need to be as detailed as possible. Detailed goals give you a specific target. In addition to including your "why", goals must also include, whenever possible, who, what, where and when.

To create a detailed goal, visualize and write it as if it already has been achieved. Writing your goal this way makes it more powerful and the goal becomes more real because you are including the outcomes.

A good example is New Year's resolutions. Do you make New Year's resolutions? If not, why? Is it because you do not want to accomplish anything in the coming year? Or is it because you have not followed through with resolutions in the past? If you have not followed through with them in the past, it might be because the goals were not strong enough. There is a good chance the resolutions did not include your "why" or any other details about achievement.

Rather than making traditional New Year's resolutions such as *"This year I am going to lose thirty pounds"*, actually *plan* your goals for the year. Instead of telling *yourself* what you *will do*, tell *someone else* what you *did* this year.

Start by envisioning it is the end of the year, December 31st, and write your goals for the year as if you are writing a letter to someone. (You probably will not mail the letter unless you want someone to help hold you accountable.) Share with them:

- What you accomplished during the year
- How you accomplished those things
- Why you accomplished them
- When you accomplished each of them
- How accomplishment felt

By doing this you are no longer telling yourself what you are going to do: *"This year I am going to lose thirty pounds";* you are telling someone else what you have done: *"This was a good year! I lost thirty pounds by the start of summer! I feel good. My clothes fit better and I am able to enjoy more activities without getting sore or tired. I accomplished this by exercising 4 – 5 times a week for 30 minutes a day, cutting out sugar, potatoes, pasta and white bread. I ate more protein, vegetables and fruit at regular intervals."* You have now made the goal more of a reality.

In the case of a grant proposal, imagine that the project is complete and write the goal from that perspective. For example: *"What a [grant project] we had. We accomplished _____, _____ and_____ . The impact(s) was _____ . We achieved all of this by _____, _____ and _____ ."*

Below are a couple more examples:

1. <u>Personal Goal</u> - Buying a New Car

   Many people might simply say, *"My goal is to buy a new car"* expecting this to be effective. Then a year down the road they still do not have a new car. Why? Because the goal was not detailed and had no "why" driving it.

17

In order for this goal to be effective, the following questions need to be answered:

- Why do I need/want a new car?
- What kind of car?
- What year is the car?
- When do I want to buy it?
- What color do I want?
- Do I want leather or cloth seats?
- What is my budget?

Answering these questions and utilizing the goal setting guidelines discussed so far, the goal might now read something like this:

*"It is October 31st and I just purchased my 2015 four-wheel drive SUV. I am very excited. My old car kept stalling, it was rusting and it was not safe on slippery roads. My new SUV is silver with tan, leather interior and it has that new car smell. My total budget was $30,000 but I got a deal when I only paid $25,000."*

2. Grant Proposal Goal - Purchasing a Digital Camera and Accessories for Your Organization

Many people might simply say, *"We plan to buy a new digital camera with software and accessories for our organization"*. This could leave evaluators asking a lot of questions. If they have questions they may deny the application.

To make this goal more effective, the following questions might be asked to clarify this proposal goal:

- Why do we want to purchase these items?
- How will the camera benefit our organization?
- Where will the camera and accessories be stored?
- Who will be using the camera? Do they have experience?

- Will we need training?
- When do we want to make the purchase?
- How will the purchase be paid for if it exceeds the grant amount?
- Where do we want to purchase the camera and accessories?

Answering some or all of these questions in the application narrative shows that the purchase was well thought out and makes your application stronger.

## Guideline #4 – *Action Plan*

Once a detailed goal has been defined and written, an action plan needs to be created. Think of the action plan as your instruction manual or recipe for success. We all need a guide, something to refer to, while we are creating something new. (See Figure 1)

The action plan needs to consist of five elements:

1. *Deadline/checkpoints*:

   The deadline needs to be realistic. If you do not allow enough time to reach it, you may give up too soon. The timeline for completing the goal by the deadline should include checkpoints where you review your progress. Example: If your ultimate deadline is eight months away maybe you check your progress once a month.

2. *Ability*:

   Take stock in your ability to reach the goal. Ask yourself questions such as:
   - What skills or knowledge do I already possess?
   - What do I need to learn?
   - How will I learn it?
   - Who do I need to enlist to help me?

When writing the goals for your grant project, explain such issues as:

- How project expenses will be paid if the grant amount is not enough to cover them. (Sponsorships, ticket sales, participant fees, other grants, cash-on-hand, etc.)
- Who will be involved in carrying out the project along with their knowledge and skills. Evaluators want to know that your organization has qualified people executing the project.
- How the community will support the project. (Volunteers, past or expected participants, etc.)

3. *Measurement*:

Define what success will look like when the goal is reached and the criteria by which success will be measured. If success is not defined, you may not know when you accomplished or exceeded the goal. Ask questions such as:

- How will achievement feel?
- How will achievement affect your life (or organization and community)?
- How will you know when the goal has been achieved?
- How will someone else know that the goal was achieved?

When clarifying your project goal(s), define success and explain how it will be evaluated and measured. Example:

- *Goal*: Increase participation over last year
- *How it will be evaluated*: Participant survey responses, ticket sales, etc.
- *Measurement*: This goal will be successfully achieved if participation is increased by 30% over last year.

4. *Manageable action steps:*

Break the goal down into smaller, more manageable action steps. List the critical things that must happen for the goal to

*Figure 1 - Goal Action Plan Tracking Chart*

| **Goal:** *(visualize as complete, include a why, be detailed)* | |
|---|---|
| **Goal Deadline:** | |
| **Anticipated Result(s), Measurement Criteria and Evaluation Tool(s) to be Used:** | |
| **Action Step** | **Action Step Deadline** |
| | |
| | |
| | |
| | |
| | |
| | |
| | |
| **Contingency Plan:** | |
| Possible Obstacles: | Solutions: |

become a reality by your ultimate deadline. Include completion dates for each step. (These dates could also be the points where you check your overall progress.)

In the previous example, buying a new car, you would list steps that need to happen to achieve the goal of owning a new car by October 31$^{st}$ (the goal deadline). Steps such as:

- Determining the cost and how the purchase will be funded
- Researching types of vehicles, sellers and insurance
- Speaking to others who have purchased vehicles and enlisting their help
- Test driving vehicles

5. *Contingency plan*:

Creating a contingency plan helps you prepare to overcome obstacles that might arise when working to achieve a goal. A contingency plan not only helps you overcome obstacles but also helps you avoid them all together because you are now aware of them.

In terms of grant writing, what is your backup plan if:

- Part of your project is an outdoor event and there is bad weather?
- An anticipated sponsorship falls through? How will you pay project expenses?
- Your project manager gets ill and cannot conduct their duties?

## Guideline #5 – *Take Action*

This guideline is self-explanatory – you need to work your plan!

- Get plugged into those things that will help you achieve the goal(s).
- Tell someone about your goal(s) who will help keep you accountable, encourage you and who will not tear you down.

- Post your goal(s) and/or individual action steps somewhere where you will see them every day.
- Take an action step(s) every day, no matter how small, toward achieving the goal(s).
- Once you have momentum, keep it going!

## *Be Flexible*

Some of your action steps may be less interesting than others are but stick to the action plan. However, you must keep in mind that nothing, including your goals, is written in stone. Be flexible and adjust the plan as needed. Flexibility opens you up to being aware of opportunities that come your way. Those opportunities could inadvertently lead you to your goals. The road from setting your goals to achievement might not be a straight line.

---

### *TIP*

If the grant application does not specifically ask questions such as *"What are the goals for the project?"*, *"How will the goals be measured?"*, *"What are the expected impacts"*, etc. share the information somewhere in the narrative to create a well thought out, complete application. It could make your application stand out over others.

---

## *Writing the Proposal Narrative*

Once the goal(s) for the project has been clarified and you can show that a project is well thought out because of the action plan(s) you created, it is time to write the proposal narrative.

As you write the narrative and answer application questions, make sure your responses are direct and clear. Remember more often than not, less is more. It is important to avoid fluff and focus on substance.

Fluff is filler information that some writers use to fill the available space. Substance is relevant information that explains the project.

Fluff occurs when, for example, a writer uses five sentences to explain an idea that could have been explained in only two sentences. The danger with fluff is that it causes the project to come across as less meritorious because the narrative does not reach the core of the proposal. It is necessary to understand that most evaluators make their decision about an application based only on the information provided within that application, not on their outside knowledge nor what they assume by "reading between the lines". This demonstrates the importance of properly defining the goals of the project and planning the action steps before you get started writing the proposal narrative. When you have done this, your responses will be direct and clear.

---

*TIP*

Have you written grant applications in the past similar to the one you are writing now? Were any of them been denied? If so, contact the grantmaking organization and ask for any feedback/critique evaluators gave during the review process. Use this information to your advantage for submitting a stronger application.

---

In a further effort to make your responses clear, strive to avoid using jargon (terminology) that is specific to your "industry" (or organization) unless you are applying for a specific type of grant in a specific genre. For example, if you are writing a grant application for a social service organization that serves the elderly and you are applying to a grantmaking organization that gives grants only to that type of organization using industry jargon would be appropriate. Evaluators would understand your responses. On the other hand, if you apply to a grantmaking organization that gives grants to different types of social service organizations it would be best to avoid industry specific jargon.

**KEEP IN MIND**

The heart of the application starts with writing detailed, measurable, well-planned goals for the project that are driven by desire and ends with clear and direct responses to application questions.

- ✓ LAY A FOUNDATION

- ✓ REVIEW THE BASICS

- ✓ CLARIFY PROPOSAL GOALS AND OUTCOMES

- ✓ WRITE A CONCISE, WELL THOUGHT OUT NARRATIVE

# CHAPTER FOUR

# PROPOSAL BUDGET AND QUOTES

D*o I always have to submit a budget with a grant application? How do I create a budget for the application?*

Depending on the grantmaking organization and grant program, you may be required to include a budget and/or quotes to support the grant request. In addition, different grantmaking organizations and evaluators have different requirements regarding the layout of the budget and quotes.

First, learn how the budget should be presented. Some grantmaking organizations and evaluators may only want a brief description of the budget included in the narrative and others may want a separate document attached to the application.

If they require a separate document, they may provide a budget page template that you will need to complete or you may have to create a budget page. If you need to create a budget page, make sure it is easy to read and understand. (See Figure 2)

Second, learn what evaluators expect to see in the budget. Do evaluators want to see only the expenses that will be paid for with grant funds or do they want to see all the expenses and revenue related to the project? If evaluators want to see only the expenses that will be paid for with grant funds, do not include any expenses that are ineligible for funding.

If evaluators want to see the entire project budget, clearly identify the expenses that will be paid for with grant funds and the expenses that will be paid for with other sources of revenue. You

*Figure 2 - Budget Page Example*

## EXPENSES

| Expense Type | Description | Expenses Paid for with Grant Funds | Expenses Paid for with Other Funds | Total |
|---|---|---|---|---|
| Personnel | Project Director 60 hrs x $15/hr | $900 | | $900 |
| | Event Speaker Contract Fee | $1,800 | | $1,800 |
| | Custodian 3 hrs x $20/hr | | $60 | $60 |
| Marketing | Newspaper Ad - 2 weeks $125 per week | $250 | | $250 |
| | 5 lunchtime Radio Spots $25 x 5 spots | $125 | | $125 |
| Lunch | $8 per person x 200 people | | $1,600 | $1,600 |
| Space Rental | 1 day | $700 | | $700 |
| Supplies | Handouts – 500 copies x $.05 per copy | $25 | | $25 |
| | 2 Flip charts $22.50 ea. | | $45 | $45 |
| **TOTAL EXPENSES** | | **$3,800** | **$1,705** | **$5,505** |

## REVENUE

| Revenue Type | Description | Total | | |
|---|---|---|---|---|
| Cash on Hand | | $355 | | |
| XYZ Company | Sponsorship – Anticipated | $350 | | |
| Giving Group | Grant – Received | $1,000 | | |
| **TOTAL REVENUE** | | **$1,705** | | |
| Grant Award | | $3,800 | | |
| **TOTAL SUPPORT** | | **$5,505** | | |

could now include the expenses that are ineligible for funding since you will be identifying them as paid with other revenue sources and they are part of the entire project budget. (Again refer to Figure 2)

Expenses and revenue sources must be clear and specific on the budget page. Example: Instead of writing "publicity" or "marketing" be more specific by listing "newspaper ads", "radio ads", or "flyers". (Keep in mind that "miscellaneous", such as "miscellaneous supplies", is typically not an accepted expense in a budget because "miscellaneous" can easily be used to pad the budget.)

In addition to being clear and specific, the expenses also need to be well explained. If you do not have room on the budget page, explain them in the narrative. You do not want the evaluators to guess about why an expense is relevant or important to the proposal.

Whenever possible show your math calculations. (Always make sure they are accurate.) Evaluators like to see how applicants came up with their totals. Examples:

- Newspaper ads 3 x $50 each
- Project manager $20/hour x 40 hours
- Participant fees $25/person x 100

---

*TIP*

Some grants that nonprofit organizations receive are for a set amount (such as $100,000 to conduct a certain type of project/incentive) and do not require a budget when applying for them. If this is the case, learn if the source of funding has any conditions on the funds. Example of a condition: Only 10% of the overall grant can be used for administrative costs such as mileage, contract personnel, staff/benefits, conference fees, hotels, etc.

---

If applying for a matching grant, a grant that requires the applicant to contribute to their own project in some way, and the match is coming from ticket sales, registration fees, donations, sponsorships, etc., attempt to also include some "cash-on-hand" funds. Evaluators like to see an organization making an investment in their own project.

## *Quotes*
*What is a quote?*

A quote is evidence of the potential purchase price of items listed in the budget. Quotes support all or part of the budget. (Generally, quotes are required when making capital purchases.) Learn from the grantmaking organization what they consider a quote. Generally, they do not accept a document that you create.

When submitting quotes with your grant application, they should be clear, concise, easy to understand and coordinate well with the budget page. Example: On the budget page you list fist a Computer, then a Printer and lastly Software, make sure the quotes you submit are in that order too. Include quotes that only show the specific items you want to purchase with the grant funds. Do not clutter the quote with other items.

---

**KEEP IN MIND**

If a grantmaking organization's staff members or evaluators have to spend a lot of time trying to make sense of your budget or quotes they may disqualify, deny or score the application low during intake or review.

- ✓ LAY A FOUNDATION

- ✓ REVIEW THE BASICS

- ✓ CLARIFY PROPOSAL GOALS AND OUTCOMES

- ✓ WRITE A CONCISE, WELL THOUGHT OUT NARRATIVE

- ✓ GENERATE A CLEAR BUDGET PAGE

# CHAPTER FIVE

# MAXIMIZING DRAFT REVIEWS

S ome grantmaking organizations have a policy that states, *"once an application is submitted, it is submitted"*. Meaning that once you submit the application you cannot make any changes. For this reason, it is essential to have others review a draft of the application before submitting it. Maximizing draft reviews is the last step to submitting the strongest application possible.

### An Evaluator's Perspective

Before asking someone else to review a draft of the application it is a good idea to:

1.  Take a break and review it with a fresh eye
2.  Double check the guidelines to make sure you addressed all of the grantmaking organization's requirements
3.  Complete the application checklist
4.  Review it from an evaluator's perspective. Ask yourself questions such as:

    *   *Is any part of the narrative confusing or incomplete?*
    *   *Do the responses appropriately address the questions asked? Are the responses direct and clear?*
    *   *Were the instructions in the guidelines and application followed?*
    *   *Does the project stand out? Does the narrative explain how the project/organization is unique or stands out over others similar to it?*

- Does the project fit with the missions of both the applicant organization and the grantmaking organization?
- *Is the need for the project explained?*
- *Does the applicant have the ability to carry out the project?*
- *Are the budget calculations accurate? Are the budget items explained?*
- *Is the project well thought out and explained?*
- *Are there any grammar or spelling issues?* Lookout for typos, missing words, repeated words, and text formatting requirements.

## *TIP*

If you are submitting the application online, it is best to use a program such as Microsoft Word to check your narrative for spelling and grammar issues. Depending on your browser, or the program used to create the online application, you might not be able to spell check your narrative properly within the application. After you have checked your document, you should be able to copy and paste your text into the online application.

## *Proofreading Tips*

A great way to proofread your application narrative (or any document) is to read it backwards. Meaning read the last paragraph or section first and work your way to the beginning of the narrative/document. You will be surprised at the things you find that you want to improve or change. You might learn that the information does not connect as well as you thought or that you repeat yourself unnecessarily. If you always read your narrative/document from the beginning, you will start to add words that should be there that are not and your editing might not be entirely accurate.

Another great tip for proofreading your narrative is to read it out loud. Reading out loud brings out errors because you will not tend to add words and confusing or "heavy" verbiage will be more noticeable.

### *Another Perspective*

After you have reviewed the draft, get another person's perspective. This person can be someone else involved in the project or a third-party not related to the project or your organization. In fact, it is a good idea to have both types of people review the draft because they will each give you a different viewpoint. Remember to provide draft reviewers with the guidelines, review criteria, final report form and your application checklist so they are able to review the application accurately.

### *Grantmaking Organization's Perspective*

In addition to another person's perspective, learn if the grantmaking organization offers a draft review service. Some organizations have staff members who will look over the application before it is submitted to help you prepare the best grant application possible for their organization. This does not guarantee funding but it can be very beneficial.

Grantmaking organizations that offer a draft review service may have draft review deadlines for each program. When you start the application process, check to see if there is such a deadline so you do not miss out on having your draft reviewed.

**KEEP IN MIND**

Submit your strongest application by maximizing draft reviews:

- Review a draft of the completed application from an evaluator's point of view
- Get another perspective by having someone else review a the draft
- Take advantage of the grantmaking organization's draft review service

✓ LAY A FOUNDATION

✓ REVIEW THE BASICS

✓ CLARIFY PROPOSAL GOALS AND OUTCOMES

✓ WRITE A CONCISE, WELL THOUGHT OUT NARRATIVE

✓ GENERATE A CLEAR BUDGET PAGE

✓ UTILIZE DRAFT REVIEWS

# CHAPTER SIX

# ADMINISTERING GRANTS

M*y application was funded! Now what?*
After a grant application has been approved, there is still work to be done. The grant must be administered (managed or overseen).

Administering a grant can be a complex job, requiring a time commitment, organization and follow through. It also requires knowing the goal(s) of the project and fulfilling the grant obligations. Some of those obligations might include:

- Using the grantmaking organization's prepared acknowledgment of the grant or logo on marketing materials or on your website
- Tracking and reporting information pertaining to the project outcomes (results)
- Properly expending grant funds on eligible project expenses and tracking/reporting those expenditures
- Retaining financial (and other) records
- Preparing for a final project audit (if applicable)

*How do I learn about my obligations?*

Some sources might be the:

- Grant contract
- Program guidelines
- Grantmaking organization's website
- Program final report form

The final report form is very useful when administering a grant. Obtaining a copy of it before starting the funded project will give you advanced notice about:

- Documents or information you will need to include with the final report such as copies of marketing materials, press releases, pictures, videos, receipts or invoices
- Statistical data you possibly will need to report such as the number of volunteers associated with the project or the number of audience members/participants (adults, children, etc.)
- Outcomes the grantmaking organization expects to be reported

### *Writing the Final Report Narrative*

To submit a strong final report at the *end* of your project, you must be collecting information *during* the project. This information will support how the project results were achieved and measured and could include:

- Participant survey responses
- Evidence of community support and involvement
- Personal stories about changes that occurred because of the project

When writing the final report narrative, start by reiterating the goal(s) of the project. Go on to explain:

- How the goal(s) was achieved (include statistics and quantitative measurements)
- Why any goals were not achieved and the lessons learned (what you would do different next time)
- What effect the project and grant funding had on your organization, the community, participants, volunteers or audience members (share personal stories you collected)
- How the community supported the project
- What type of partnerships were developed with other

organizations or businesses during the project and why those partnerships were important to the project and/or future projects

## *Reporting Expenditures*

If a budget is required with the final report, learn if the grantmaking organization requires only a brief description of the budget be included in the narrative or if they require a separate budget page be attached to the final report. If a separate budget page needs to be attached, is a budget page template provided or are you required to create one.

If you are required to create a final report budget page, it must be easy to read and should compare the *proposal* budget numbers with the *actual* project expenditures. (See Figure 3) If the *actual* project expenditures are different from the *proposal* budget numbers, explain the change in the final report narrative. A couple of tips:

- The total expenses must match the total revenues.
- If you must include receipts for purchases, be sure they are well organized and correlate with the budget page.

## *The Importance of Reporting*

As mentioned in chapter one, typically grantmaking organizations receive the funds they disperse to their constituents from an outside source. When the funds come from an outside source, the grantmaking organization has an obligation to report on the:

- Disbursement of those funds
- Project outcomes
- Impacts those funds had on other organizations and community members

Further funding from the source may be dependent on this reporting.

*Figure 3 - Final Report Budget Page Example*

| EXPENSES | | |
|---|---|---|
| **Expense Type** | **Proposal Budget Totals** | **Actual Expenditures** |
| Personnel | $2,760 | $2,850 |
| Marketing | $375 | $375 |
| Lunch | $1,600 | $1,650 |
| Space Rental | $700 | $700 |
| Supplies | $70 | $35 |
| **TOTAL EXPENSES** | **$5,505** | **$5,610** |
| **REVENUE TYPE** | | |
| Cash on Hand | $355 | $810 |
| XYZ Company – Sponsorship | $350 | $0 |
| Giving Group – Grant | $1,000 | $1,000 |
| **TOTAL REVENUE** | **$1,705** | **$1,810** |
| Grant Award | $3,800 | $3,800 |
| **TOTAL SUPPORT** | **$5,505** | **$5,610** |

---

### KEEP IN MIND

By submitting all progress/final reports by the deadlines and supplying as much information as possible about your project outcomes, you will be assisting the grantmaking organization to meet their reporting obligations as well as increasing your organization's eligibility for future grant funding through the grantmaking organization.

- ✓ LEARN OBLIGATIONS

- ✓ COLLECT INFORMATION

- ✓ EXPEND GRANT FUNDS ON ELIGIBLE EXPENSES

- ✓ TRACK AND REPORT EXPENDITURES AND REVENUE

- ✓ REPORT PROJECT OUTCOMES BY DEADLINE

# CONCLUSION

Grants are a great source of support, they can be highly competitive and nothing can guarantee funding of a grant application. For these reasons, the ability to submit a strong grant application is valuable. Submitting a strong application starts with understanding the granting process and the expectations of grantmaking organizations/evaluators and ends with writing a clear and concise proposal narrative.

The main goals of *Effective Grant Writing: Submit a Stronger Application* were to answer commonly asked questions about the grant process and to give real examples of setting/explaining proposal goals and developing an application budget. Most of the information provided in *Effective Grant Writing: Submit a Stronger Application* boils down to four elements:

1. Preparing in advance
2. Creating a well thought out narrative
3. Avoiding common mistakes
4. Reinforcing your work

The first three elements are tied together and revolve around advanced preparation. The work you do *before* writing the proposal narrative is just as important as actually writing it. This preparation leads to creating a well thought out proposal and helps you avoid some of the common mistakes. Advanced preparation includes:

- Reading the program guidelines to get educated about the program
- Learning the application basics for the program
- Using the final report form to look at the expected end-result

- Clarifying and planning the goals/outcomes for the project
- Noting the application deadline and any draft review deadline

All of your work in preparing the proposal is reinforced when you utilize your application checklist and maximize the use of draft reviews.

*Now it is time to write and submit your best application. Good luck in your grant writing adventures!*

# ABOUT THE AUTHOR

**A**ngie R. Boecker is a graduate of the St. Cloud Business College. For over seven years, she was the Grants Specialist for a grantmaking organization. She was involved in developing grant programs funded by the McKnight Foundation and the Minnesota State Legislature. She conducted intake on submitted grant applications ensuring applicant eligibility, guideline compliance and application completeness. She was also in charge of reporting constituent/project statistical data and grant impacts to the Minnesota State Arts Board.

In addition, Angie was a Minnesota Intelligent Rural Community Coordinator with a County Economic Development Department, where she co-managed the County's part in C.K. Blandin Foundation's broadband initiative in partnership with the University of Minnesota Extension. In this role, she was involved in managing the project budget, acted as a liaison between the economic development department and project contractors, reported about project outcomes and impacts and prepared for the final project audit.

Currently, Angie conducts private and group trainings where she strives to deliver thought provoking messages that will inspire audience members to take action. Angie tailors her trainings to the capacity building and development needs of non-profit organizations or businesses as well as individual personal development.

www.EliteTrainingetc.com

www.facebook.com/AngieRBoeckerETC

www.ingramcontent.com/pod-product-compliance
Lightning Source LLC
Chambersburg PA
CBHW050540210326
41520CB00012B/2648